Tragic Truth

Flesh: The Heart that Stood Still

I

I'll love the thought of you, of us.

    Though, I love the thought of happiness more.

        -Jeremiah Thy Poet

II

I am my own worst critic;

    I critique my final ideas...

        my never-ending emotions,

            my abstract self-portrait.

My mental state is at the point of no return.

    Though, I learn to find a moral compass.

        -Jeremiah Thy Poet

III

I am

    chasing

        my own demons

over and over again...

Let's pretend I found them and that I'll be just fine.

        -Jeremiah Thy Poet

IV

Before your eyes see

       hear for the wind in the trees...

           thank the sky to breathe.

-Jeremiah Thy Poet

V

As the wishing well

       drowns my dreams

these copper coins will

           continue to sink.

These hopeful sorrows will wash away

       to exist another day,

haunting me I'll never be set free.

As the wishing well drowns my dreams,

         I will continue to lose my sleep...

-Jeremiah Thy Poet

VI

I am from a pale white horse

    and a religious goddess,

        from roots above and branches below.

I am from sin that's waiting for faith to begin;

    from dreams that are longing for too much...

I am from depression skies and a world of lies,

    from empty hearts that keep falling apart.

-Jeremiah Thy Poet

VII

He doesn't promise an explanation...

    Where did I start breathing,

        Where did I first open my eyes,

            Where did I let my tears fall first?

The gates of hell opened up when I started crawling,

    crawling towards forgiveness...

I have been a slave of sin when I started walking,

    walking everywhere...

I have been lost and found by tragic times

    disguised as hope and faith,

        to remain sane.

Pray for you and me...

-Jeremiah Thy Poet

VIII

I don't belong
> here or there.

Where do I go
> from down here to up there?

> *-Jeremiah Thy Poet*

IX

As the heavens unfolded before him
> he beheld the mind-set of isolation
>> only to be discovered in a series of hesitation.

As hell followed he gained solitude,
> rich in shame and humility;
>> a throne for the unforgiving, for the unknown.

He offered his set of eyes to the sky in prayer that everything will be just fine...
> waiting for the last moment to endure the thought of nothing.

> *-Jeremiah Thy Poet*

X

A broken heart is flesh,

it will heal.

A soul is abstract...

Its wounds are far too severe to heal.

 I am damaged through experience.

 -Jeremiah Thy Poet

XI

As I breathe in the today

 my mind ponders on tomorrow.

 As I lay awake trying to define my thinking.

Thoughts in reverse,

 emotions in rehearse;

 body in balance.

As I breathe lying awake on this night I find myself at a stand still...

the heart that stood still;

reflect,

reflecting,

reflection.

I question why I cannot sleep...

 piece by piece I will find peace, true peace.

 -Jeremiah Thy Poet

XII

For the time being

    while you were in my heart,

        your eyes provided light.

A sense of stillness that I couldn't escape from...

-Jeremiah Thy Poet

XIII

My love for you has traveled to a destination...

    Let's end this chapter and go our different ways

        for our hearts are not in the same place.

-Jeremiah Thy Poet

XIV

You and I walk different paths.

    How long can you last in mine?

My mental state is barricaded

    formed into an asylum,

        with emotions too much of a burden

            so I hide them.

-Jeremiah Thy Poet

XV

Should I wait here for something to happen?

I stand here corrected now.

    Take my hand,

        breathe with me,

           and embrace us.

Don't let go of what we were and let go of what we weren't.

-Jeremiah Thy Poet

XVI

I have been lost and found

        by many...

A boy who was an abandoned outcast.

He fell through the heavens finding lost times.

    As he waited for the unexpected to be known,

        moments began to unfold...

-Jeremiah Thy Poet

XVII

I'm defeating the purpose
    by writing my thoughts,
        these words.
You and I walk different paths.
    How long can I last in yours?

-Jeremiah Thy Poet

XVIII

Slave of Sin...
    If only, if only i could reach the heavens just to feel safe
        and still be able to walk and remain on hells dirt,
            to feel that I'm at home.

I'm mentally exhausted, breathing...
    my heart is beating itself alive
        overwhelmed trying to survive,
          with emotions wanting to die.
This is it, my time to rise.
    Can I make it out alive for I am just trying to survive.

-Jeremiah Thy Poet

XIX

Everything is now a reflection.

    I was stuck in your mentality,

        your logic...

I casted mirrors to save my life.

    We both hurt now.

        Timeline; deadline

-Jeremiah Thy Poet

XX

I was devoted,

    I was doomed...

        I assumed that our love was sincerely true.

-Jeremiah Thy Poet

XXI

These thoughts blame themselves.

I'm falling to a place where I dwell.

Looking both ways

    I can never tell

If it's heaven or hell.

    Just know I'm on my way.

-Jeremiah Thy Poet

XXII

I got no time for puzzles,

        the struggle finds me.

I put that together

        whether you know it or not.

-Jeremiah Thy Poet

Mind: Avoid to Avoid

I

I am hopelessly lost in a void,

        trying to escape.

    The rhythm of my heartbeat distracts my restless mind.

        My soul will forever be trapped in this deep void of mine.

To be set free is just a contradiction of my forever dream…

        to be set free is just a false dream.

When will I wake to be casted out from this illusion?

-Jeremiah Thy Poet

II

I followed the momentum of the devils thought process;

    He made me choose to sink or swim.

        I was lost swimming and exhausted... drowning.

-Jeremiah Thy Poet

III

My eyes see enough,

    my heart feels too much.

Nothing is what as it seems;

    This life is a false dream for a restless soul, my soul.

Time to let it all go.

-Jeremiah Thy Poet

IV

… and no one saved him

        as he was sinking.

Finally, his body gave into the overwhelming fear of exhaustion

        that became of him...

-Jeremiah Thy Poet

V

I believe in broken hearts

        because mine keeps falling apart.

-Jeremiah Thy Poet

VI

There were those moments again drowning inside my head.

        I must dream another dream.

To let go of these memories with you in mind.

Here I go again trapped inside my head.

        As I crawl out of this insanity,

        this time I'll take away the things I wanted to say

        with you in mind.

I'll run away from a place

        that we called home.

        Where you left me all alone...

-Jeremiah Thy Poet

VII

How I appreciate the feeling that everything will be just fine.

    It is true

        it's so not true

           so undeniably untrue.

Here I go again trapped inside my head.

                How can this be, how will I be set free?

-Jeremiah Thy Poet

VIII

I'm leaving in silence.

    My words in my mind start to wake,

        turns and grows into voices I dread to escape.

I cannot explain nor understand what they say...

        I just tell myself to live through another day.

I pray

    and

      I pray

in a quiet manner because most of the time

        I feel like it wouldn't matter.

I suppress this warm anxiety in my chest,

        to not feed these demons

          that live there and choose to rest.

-Jeremiah Thy Poet

IX

Don't look into my eyes...

        I can only see a blur.

I can only speak of words

        that doesn't make sense.

I try to pretend

        that I breathe in relaxation

           when I'm breathing in thoughts of humiliation.

I lapse, relapse, and lapse

        in the back of my mind

           making the twelve steps to move forward

        although, my mind is constantly on rewind

           making a discovery that I'm trying to drown myself into recovery.

I'm just trying to drown these bad and false memories.

-Jeremiah Thy Poet

X

Mental health is tricky...

        it's like a yesterday

           breathing in today.

However, wanting to leave bye tomorrow.

-Jeremiah Thy Poet

XI

Your eyes

      are hollow

            they follow

                a false fantasy

                    within me...

You turned me

      inside out,

upside down.

My eyes are set

      to haunt and kill my own demons.

-Jeremiah Thy Poet

XII

If only...

    Eye to eye

        you and I have met once too many times.

You and I have quarreled in questioning of each others fond memories;

Life is but a dream,

    life is not what it may seem.

Anxiety survives in this mind of mine,

    with emotions too unkind.

Reflections drowning in my eyes...

    Until we meet again or against my odd times,

        or my odd moments in life.

My friend, my enemy... Death.

-Jeremiah Thy Poet

Spirit: A Soul to Find

I

I sin everyday,

I'm blessed everyday;

> As I live to comprehend life everyday that would make me a saint.

Heaven or Hell, I'll be a soul that's blessed and cursed.

-Jeremiah Thy Poet

II

Physically I'll go extinct;

> My existence will be buried alive.

Mentally, I'll be set free in a maze...

> The Underworld will hold my mind captive.

My soul without hesitation will keep living without the elements of life.

The gates of hell will cage the great as I am.

> I'll keep traveling in moments, dead or alive.

-Jeremiah Thy Poet

III

My existence is not found within

my anatomy,

my mind,

my soul...

though with others that hold and carry on the true memories of me;

the great I am... lifeless.

-Jeremiah Thy Poet

IV

When life seems so difficult, just comprehend and learn that it's a challenge we face. Allow moments of reflection to guide you with whatever you are trying to achieve.

Live for your passion, don't live for your self-destructive mindset.

-Jeremiah Thy Poet

V

My mind, body, and soul has birthed a new heart for another, and her name is Life.

-Jeremiah Thy Poet

VI

Reflection within mind only to find a rhythm, a rhythm of you...

-Jeremiah Thy Poet

VII

My body is a temple; my soul, never-ending...

-Jeremiah Thy Poet

VIII

There were many that doubted me...
   I am the author of my life.
My words, sentences, paragraphs, and chapters are lived by me.
      My self-worth is dependent on the great I am.

-Jeremiah Thy Poet

IX

Bless me My Love

    I have came to my senses,

        this distance has me going reckless...

          remembrance has me going restless.

              Bless me My Love.

-Jeremiah Thy Poet

X

My words

    drown

        my soul.

They find

    me

     in my darkest

         hours;

the seconds

    I suffer,

the minutes

    I miss,

the hours

    I wish I could

       hide from.

How can I find rest

    in my darkest times?

-Jeremiah Thy Poet

45149500R00015

A child who was born to become a learning adolescent only to discover a hidden dark talent through tragedy by written poems and short stories as a teenager, now an adult has released his words...

ISBN 9798505644362

90000

9 798505 644362

COMO YO

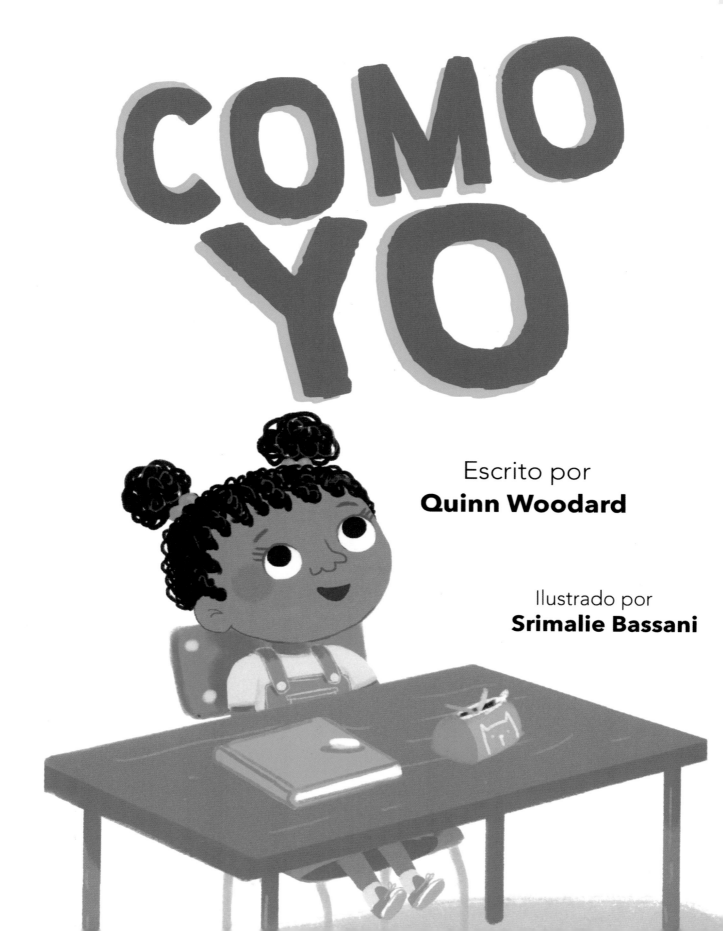

Escrito por
Quinn Woodard

Ilustrado por
Srimalie Bassani